Storm Approaching!

Kathleen Weidner Zoehfeld

RANDOM HOUSE 🏠 NEW YORK

p. i © Richard Valdez/Alamy Stock Photo; p. 8 © John Sazaklis; p. 9 courtesy of NASA; p. 13 © sandro lacarbona/Alamy Stock Photo; pp. 14, 15, 16, 18, and 21 courtesy of NASA; p. 24 © Image Source/Alamy Stock Photo; p. 25 courtesy of NASA; p. 27 © Michael Caiati; p. 29 © David R. Frazier Photolibrary, Inc./Alamy Stock Photo; p. 30 © Greg Balfour Evans/Alamy Stock Photo; p. 31 courtesy of NOAA; p. 32 © imageBROKER/Alamy Stock Photo; p. 33 © Anne Saarinen/Alamy Stock Photo; p. 35 © Marcus Harrison - plants/Alamy Stock Photo; p. 36 © ACnoncc/Alamy Stock Photo; p. 37 © Ian Shaw/Alamy Stock Photo; p. 38 (top) © Jeff J Daly/Alamy Stock Photo; p. 38 (bottom) © Chuck Eckert/Alamy Stock Photo; p. 39 © Enviroman/Alamy Stock Photo; p. 40 (top) © Steffen Hauser/botanikfoto/Alamy Stock Photo; p. 40 (bottom) © Simon Belcher/Alamy Stock Photo; p. 42 © imageBROKER/Alamy Stock Photo; p. 43 © David R. Frazier Photolibrary, Inc./Alamy Stock Photo; p. 44 © Ian Sheppard/Alamy Stock Photo; p. 45 courtesy of NASA; p. 46 © T.M.O.Pictures/Alamy Stock Photo; p. 49 courtesy of NOAA; p. 51 © Richard Valdez/Alamy Stock Photo; p. 53 © Ryan McGinnis/Alamy Stock Photo; p. 54 © James Thew/Alamy Stock Photo; pp. 56 and 57 courtesy of NOAA; p. 60 © Martin Lisius/Alamy Stock Photo; p. 61 © NG Images/Alamy Stock Photo; p. 62 © FBI Photo/Alamy Stock Photo; p. 65 © Michael Fitzsimmons/Alamy Stock Photo; p. 66 courtesy NOAA/Department of Commerce; p. 70 © 615 collection/Alamy Stock Photo; p. 72 courtesy of Wil von Dauster, NOAA; p. 73 © AlessandraRCstock/Alamy Stock Photo; p. 75 © Photo Researchers, Inc./Alamy Stock Photo; p. 76 © Matt Purciel/Alamy Stock Photo

Published in the United States by Random House Children's Books, a division of Penguin Random House LLC, New York.

Random House and the colophon are registered trademarks of Penguin Random House LLC.

Visit us on the Web! randomhousekids.com

Educators and librarians, for a variety of teaching tools, visit us at RHTeachersLibrarians.com

Library of Congress Cataloging-in-Publication Data is available upon request.

ISBN 978-1-101-93343-5 (trade) — ISBN 978-1-101-93344-2 (lib. bdg.) — ISBN 978-1-101-93345-9 (ebook)

Printed in the United States of America

10 9 8 7 6 5 4 3 2 1

Contents

Note to Readers

What do dragons have to do with real-life science and history?
More than you might think!

For thousands of years, cultures all over the world have told stories about dragons, just as they told fanciful tales about unicorns, fairies, mermaids, ogres, and other mythical creatures. People made up these and other legends for many reasons: to explain the natural world, to give their lives deeper meaning, sometimes even just for fun! Stories passed down from generation to generation began to change over time. In many cases, fact (what's true) and fiction (what's made up) blended together to create a rich legacy of storytelling.

So even though you don't see them flying overhead, dragons are all around us! They are a part of our history and culture, bridging the gap between the past and the present — what's real and what's born of our limitless imaginations. This makes the *DreamWorks Dragons* Dragon Riders ideal candidates to teach us about our world!

Think of the School of Dragons series as your treasure map to a land of fascinating facts about science, history, mythology, culture, innovation, and more! You can read the books cover to cover or skip around to sections that most interest you. There's no right or wrong way when it comes to learning.

And that's not all! When you're done reading the books, you can go online to schoolofdragons.com to play the interactive School of Dragons video games from JumpStart. There's no end to what you can discover.

All ready? Hold on tight, dragon trainers! Here we go. . . .

Meet the Characters

Astrid

Hiccup

Snotlout

Fishlegs

Stoick the Vast

Gobber

Ruffnut & Tuffnut

Meet the Dragons

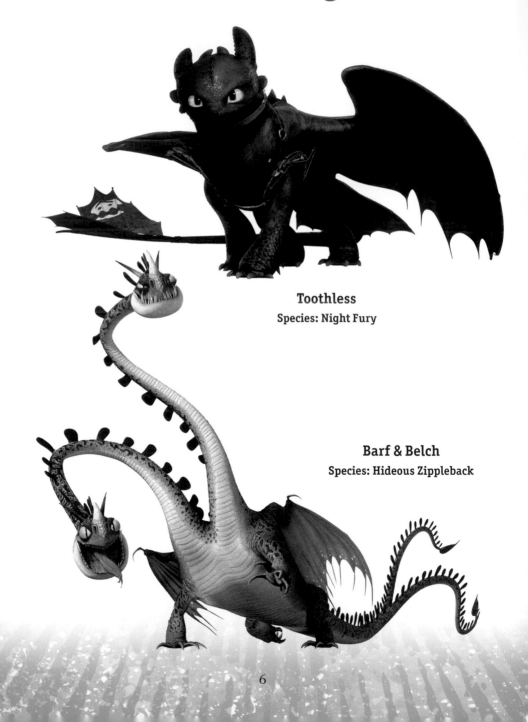

Toothless

Species: Night Fury

Barf & Belch

Species: Hideous Zippleback

Hookfang

Species: Monstrous Nightmare

Meatlug

Species: Gronckle

Stormfly

Species: Deadly Nadder

Where Weather Happens

Look up into the sky. Is it blue today? Are there puffy white clouds floating overhead? Or does the whole sky look dull and gray?

A sunny day in Chios, Greece

You're probably already pretty good at guessing what the weather will be just by looking out the window. A blue sky likely means a sunny day. And if the sky is gray, you'd better find your umbrella!

Warm or cold, rainy or clear—whatever the weather will be, it all happens in Earth's atmosphere. The **atmosphere** is the envelope of air that surrounds the Earth. It's made up of a mixture of gases, mainly nitrogen and oxygen. The atmosphere gives us the air we need to breathe. It works like a comfortable blanket, making sure Earth is never too hot or too cold to support life. It also shields living things from dangerous rays from the sun.

Earth's atmosphere

When we look up at the clouds, they seem far away. The sky seems huge—almost endless—to us below. But compared to the size of the Earth, the atmosphere is only a very small layer. If you shrank the Earth to the size of a beach ball, the atmosphere would be thinner than a sheet of paper!

Like all things on Earth, the gases in the atmosphere are made up of extremely tiny particles called atoms and molecules. In solids and liquids, the atoms and molecules tend to stick together. But in gases, they stay farther apart. They jiggle and wiggle and bounce around very easily.

Close to the Earth, the air is **dense.** All the tiny molecules that make up the air are pressed close together. At the surface of the Earth, the atmosphere squeezes down on everything.

LET'S DO A LITTLE MATH. The pressure of the atmosphere can change, but it averages about 14.7 pounds per square inch. Say the top of your head is around 25 square inches. 14.7 pounds x 25 square inches = 367.5 pounds. Three hundred sixty-seven and a half pounds! That's how hard the atmosphere is pushing on the top of your head. If you put a weight that heavy on your head, you'd surely notice it! But we don't notice the pressure of the atmosphere. It's what we're used to!

367.5 pounds isn't heavy for a Viking!

Toothless and I fly over Berk's beautiful mountains.

As you climb a high mountain or take off in an airplane, you may feel your ears pop. That's because the air pressure decreases as you go up. The tiny molecules of air are getting farther and farther apart.

As you go higher and higher, the air begins to feel colder, too. At the bottom of the mountain, you may start your hike in shorts and a T-shirt.

Mount Everest

But you'll need long pants and a jacket by the time you reach the top!

Mount Everest, in Nepal, is the tallest mountain in the world. At the top, the air is very thin. The molecules of air are very far apart. There are only about one-third as many air molecules per cubic inch as there are at the bottom of the mountain. People who climb super-high mountains often bring tanks of oxygen along with them, so they have enough air to breathe!

Jet planes can fly a kilometer or two higher than the world's highest mountains. Any higher than that and there is not enough air to keep an airplane up. No one can live that high up, either, unless they stay in a spacecraft or space suit.

There is no firm line to mark exactly where our atmosphere ends and outer space begins. The air molecules just get farther and farther apart. At around 6,200 miles (10,000 kilometers), there are only a few molecules escaping forever into space.

An astronaut needs a space suit to survive in space.

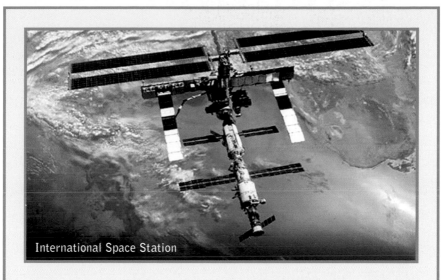

International Space Station

HOW HIGH IS TOO HIGH? The International Space Station orbits the Earth at a height of about 248 miles (400 kilometers). Astronauts who live there need a special life-support system. This gives them plenty of oxygen, and it filters the station's air to keep it clean.

Almost all the Earth's weather happens in the bottom layer of the atmosphere—the **troposphere.** The troposphere reaches a little higher than usual at the **equator** and a little lower than usual at the North and South Poles. It averages about 7.5 miles (12 kilometers) thick. Some clouds and winds can form slightly higher still—in the **stratosphere.** If you go higher than 20 miles (32 kilometers), you'll find there is no weather at all!

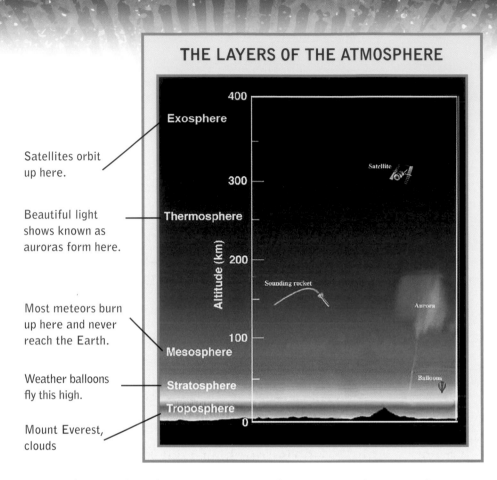

THE LAYERS OF THE ATMOSPHERE

Exosphere

Satellites orbit up here.

Thermosphere

Beautiful light shows known as auroras form here.

Altitude (km)

Satellite

Sounding rocket

Aurora

Most meteors burn up here and never reach the Earth.

Mesosphere

Weather balloons fly this high.

Stratosphere

Balloons

Troposphere

Mount Everest, clouds

The only thing certain about weather is that it will change! The atmosphere is always in motion. You can feel and see it. Maybe it's just a cool breeze on your skin at the end of a hot, still day. Or suddenly tree branches start swaying. Dark clouds form where there was blue sky just moments before. What power drives our constantly changing weather?

Heat from the Sun

Everyone loves a sunny day. When you play outdoors, you can feel the warmth of the sun's rays. If it gets too hot, try to find a shady spot. It'll be much cooler there!

Most of the sun's rays pass through the atmosphere. They warm the surface of the Earth. The atmosphere holds much of that heat in.

So the sun heats the Earth. But it heats the Earth unevenly—and that is the key to our always-changing weather. Most areas near the equator are hot all year round. If you live near the North or South Pole, prepare to keep your coat and mittens on full-time! That's because the Earth is shaped like a giant ball. At the equator, the sun's rays hit

How the Sun's Rays Hit the Earth

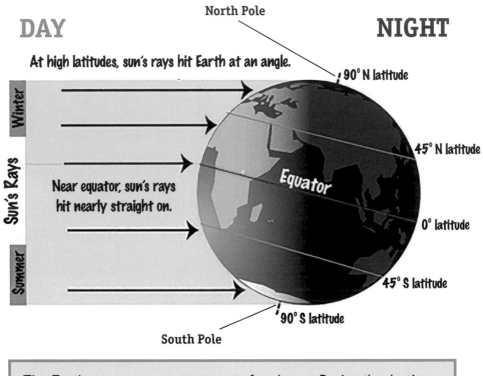

DAY

North Pole

NIGHT

At high latitudes, sun's rays hit Earth at an angle.

90° N latitude

Winter

45° N latitude

Sun's Rays

Equator

Near equator, sun's rays hit nearly straight on.

0° latitude

45° S latitude

Summer

90° S latitude

South Pole

> The Earth rotates once every twenty-four hours. During the daytime, the areas of Earth in sunlight warm up. At night, those areas cool off.

Earth directly. At the poles, they hit the Earth at an angle. Direct rays heat the Earth more intensely than slanted rays do. Uneven heating of the Earth causes uneven heating of the atmosphere.

Uneven heating keeps our atmosphere in constant motion. The molecules in cold air move around more slowly and are more closely packed together. Cold air is dense and heavy. As air heats up, the molecules move faster and spread farther apart. Heated air becomes lighter and less dense. That means warmer air tends to rise and cooler air tends to sink.

The air near the equator gets a lot of heat from the sun. As the air soaks up heat, it becomes lighter. It rises up.

Near the North and South Poles, the air is always getting chilled. The cooling air becomes heavier and sinks.

Warm air from the equator rushes toward the poles as it rises, and the cooling polar air blows toward the equator as it sinks.

This is the main way uneven heating drives the Earth's winds. These moving winds cause changing weather all around the globe. But Earth's winds don't simply blow straight from the equator to the poles and back. Because the Earth spins, or rotates, like a top, those winds are always being pushed sideways.

THE CORIOLIS FORCE

The Earth rotates from west to east. All points on Earth make one rotation every twenty-four hours. A point on the equator has to speed along at about 1,037 miles per hour (1,670 kilometers per hour) to make one rotation. A point on the **Arctic Circle** or **Antarctic Circle** only has to move at about 413 miles per hour (664 kilometers per hour) to make one rotation. That difference in speed causes winds to be pushed toward the east in the **Northern Hemisphere** and toward the west in the **Southern Hemisphere.** This pushing on the atmosphere caused by Earth's rotation is called the **Coriolis force.**

The constant flow of warm and cold air between the equator and the North and South Poles is very important. It helps propel Earth's major winds. Other factors can affect the temperature of the atmosphere, too. Large bodies of water warm up and cool off more slowly than land does. Lands covered in green forests absorb a lot of the sun's energy because of their dark color. Snow-covered white areas mostly reflect the sun instead of absorbing heat. Big mountain ranges block winds and can force them up or down slopes.

Different areas experience their own winds. And day after day, those winds bring changing weather.

Right now, all over the Earth, huge masses of cold air and warm air are meeting and pushing each other around. When a warm air mass meets a cold air mass near you, you will surely know it! Can you guess what will happen?

In the daytime, the sun warms the water and the land. The land warms up faster than the water. The air over the land gets warm faster, too. The warm air rises. The cooler air over the water blows in to take its place.

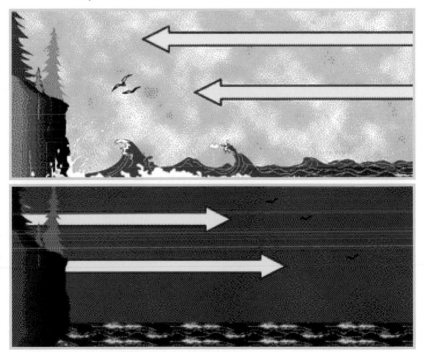

At night, the land cools off more quickly than the water. Now the air over the water is warmer than the air over the land. As the air rises, the cooler air from the land blows in to take its place.

When we go to the beach on sunny days, the water feels cooler than the sand.

How to Compare Cold Air to Hot Air

YOU'LL NEED:

TWO BOWLS • ICE WATER • HOT WATER •
A BALLOON • A PLASTIC WATER OR SODA BOTTLE •
MEASURING TAPE

Fill one bowl with ice water and the other with hot water. Blow up the balloon about halfway. Slip the end of the balloon over the opening of the bottle. Hold the bottle firmly in the hot water for five minutes. Use the measuring tape to measure the balloon around its widest part.

Then, with the balloon still in place, move the bottle to the ice water. Hold it there for five minutes. Measure the balloon again the same way. Did the measurement change?

Here's what's happening: The hot water heats the air in the bottle. As the air gets warmer, it becomes less dense. The same amount of air takes up more space. The warm air rises up into the balloon, and the balloon expands.

The cold water cools the air in the bottle. The air becomes denser, and it takes up less space. The cooler air sinks back down into the bottle, and the balloon shrinks.

Rain and Snow and Sleet

Wherever warm and cold air masses meet, there will be weather! What kind of weather? Well, that depends on how fast the local air masses are moving compared to one another. It also depends on the amount of **water vapor** in the air. Water vapor is water in the form of a gas.

Dry air is made up of a mixture of different gases, and nowhere on Earth is the air completely dry. Even over the driest deserts, like the Sahara in Africa, the air holds at least some water vapor. Water vapor is one of the most important gases in the atmosphere when it comes to weather.

Sahara Desert

Dry Air: What's in the Mix?

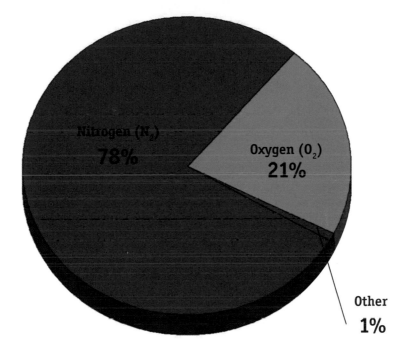

Nitrogen (N_2)
78%

Oxygen (O_2)
21%

Other
1%

The remaining 1% includes carbon dioxide (CO_2), argon (Ar), methane (CH_4), ozone (O_3), and countless tiny particles of soot, ash, and dust.

Water vapor gets into the air through **evaporation.** You may have experimented with this before in one of your science classes. Put a dish of water in a sunny place. In a day or two, the water is gone. You know it hasn't just disappeared! The **energy** of the sun excited the water molecules in your dish. They bounced around faster and faster until they all left the dish and spread out into the air. This is called evaporation. It's the process of changing from liquid into gas. Evaporation doesn't happen just in a dish in your classroom. Every day, water evaporates from the surface of the ocean, lakes, and streams. The water molecules rise into the air as water vapor. In warm, wet areas, lots of water evaporates. In freezing-cold places, much less does.

Water vapor leaves the air through **condensation**. Condensation is the process of changing from a gas into a liquid. Warm air can hold more water vapor than cool air can. We already know that warm air tends to rise. As this happens, the air becomes colder. Since cold air cannot hold as much moisture as warm air, the water vapor begins to turn back into liquid water. It turns into tiny water droplets. If the temperature is cold enough, the water vapor turns into tiny ice crystals. The clouds you see overhead are made up of countless droplets of water and crystals of ice.

CONDENSATION IN ACTION

It's easy to see how condensation works. Fill a glass with ice water on a warm day. Within minutes, droplets of water will be forming on the outside of your glass.

The ice water cools your glass. The glass cools the air around it. As the air cools, the water vapor in the air turns into droplets of liquid water. If the air is very moist, those droplets will grow bigger. Drops of water will soon be running down the side of your glass!

Water vapor always needs something on which to condense. Water droplets condense on the outside of your glass. In the atmosphere, droplets condense around tiny particles of dust, ash, and soot. And that's how clouds form!

It's fun to look up and watch the clouds moving and changing in the sky. Different kinds of clouds bring different kinds of weather. But almost all clouds form where warm and cold air masses meet. The area where two air masses meet is called a **front.** You may have heard

Belch and Barf are a powerful dragon front!

Meteorologist at work

meteorologists on the news mention "cold fronts" and "warm fronts" when they are reporting on the weather.

Sometimes a fast-moving cold air mass pushes under a warm air mass. This is known as a **cold front**. The cold air makes the warm air rise quickly. Where the warmer air rises over the cold air, billowy clouds begin to build. The tops of the clouds reach up, higher and higher. The clouds grow dark and heavy.

At other times, a warm air mass may move in over a cold air mass. This is known as a **warm front.** The warm air slowly rises over the cool air. Broad, sheet-like clouds build gradually where the two masses meet.

Cumulus clouds

All clouds have at least one of three basic shapes. Some are a combination of two.

Cumulus clouds look like giant, puffy cotton balls.

Meatlug looks like a giant puffy cumulus cloud!

Usually blue sky can be seen between the clouds. If conditions are right, they can build to form huge cumulonimbus clouds, whose tops reach up to seven miles (eleven kilometers) above the Earth's surface. Heavy rain or snow often falls from cumulonimbus clouds. Thunderstorms are born in the biggest cumulonimbus clouds.

Stratus clouds are broad and thin, and they hang low in the sky. Stratus clouds can make the whole sky look white or gray. Drizzly rain or sleet may fall from them if they become thick enough. A very low-forming stratus cloud is known as fog.

Stratus clouds

Cirrus clouds

Cirrus clouds are high, wispy clouds made up of ice crystals. Rain doesn't fall from cirrus clouds, but they're often a sign that air masses are on the move. If you see cirrus clouds, there is a good chance that unsettled or rainy weather is soon to come.

Clouds are made up of tiny droplets of water that have condensed from the air. But not every cloud brings rain. Any water that falls to the ground from clouds—whether in the form of rain, sleet, or snow—is called **precipitation.**

We have some pretty bad snow and sleet here in Berk at times. It makes dragon flying almost impossible!

What is it that turns a cloudy day into a day with precipitation? In warm clouds, the droplets of water are bouncing all around. The water droplets are held up by the air currents, or winds, within the clouds. As the droplets bounce around, some of them collide and stick together. They get bigger and bigger, until they are heavy enough to fall as rain. If the rain falls through a layer of very cold air, the raindrops freeze and turn into **sleet** on the way down.

Snow and sleet

In cold clouds, tiny ice crystals form through a process similar to condensation. Water vapor in the clouds begins to condense on the ice crystals, and the crystals grow. Beautiful, six-sided snow crystals, called **snowflakes,** begin to form. Soon the snowflakes become so heavy they start to fall. If they fall through cold air, the snow on the ground will be light and fluffy and great for sleigh riding. If the snowflakes fall through warmer air, they may begin to melt on the way down. Then you'll have a wet, sloppy snow—the kind that soaks through your clothes! If the air is very warm, the snow may melt completely and turn into rain by the time it reaches the ground.

Look up at the sky. Do you think there will be some precipitation today? If you're not sure, you can always check the weather report.

HOW MANY DROPLETS MAKE A DROP?

Close-up of raindrops

It takes at least one million cloud droplets to make up a raindrop that is heavy enough to fall. Drizzly rain has the smallest raindrops. An average-size raindrop may form from as many as ten million droplets.

On days when it seems to be "raining cats and dogs," those raindrops are not really as big as cats or dogs. But they are pretty big!

What Will the Weather Be?

Maybe you have a picnic planned for Saturday. Or you're going to a football game on Sunday afternoon. It's always nice to know what the weather will be! To find out, you can turn to a weather channel on your TV or use a weather app on your computer or smartphone.

Weather forecast on a smartphone

Where do these weather reports come from? Meteorologists are scientists who study the weather. They observe changes in the atmosphere and keep track of those changes over time.

Scientists have set up weather stations in thousands of places all around the globe. Each of these stations has a set of basic tools to help measure the weather in specific areas.

A pinwheel-like anemometer to measure wind speed

A hygrometer to measure water vapor, or humidity, in the air

A barometer to keep track of changes in air pressure

A weather vane to show the direction of the wind

Meteorologists name winds for the direction from which they come. For example, a wind that blows from east to west is an east wind, or an easterly.

A rain gauge to measure how much rain there has been

A thermometer to check the air temperature

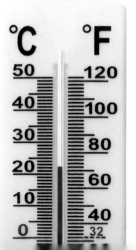

SET UP YOUR OWN WEATHER STATION

Check out the National Oceanic and Atmospheric Administration's link to find out how to build your own weather station! oceanservice.noaa.gov/education/for_fun /BuildyourownWeatherStation.pdf

How Pressure Affects the Weather

If a weather report says you're in a **low-pressure system,** that means there is a lot of warm air rising around you. A low-pressure reading on a barometer means clouds and precipitation could be showing up soon.

A **high-pressure system** happens when air at the center of the system is sinking quickly. A high-pressure reading on a barometer usually means you're in for some dry and stable weather.

We're anything but stable!

Meteorologists can get information from weather stations almost instantly. Information from local weather stations forms the basis of the daily weather report. But how do meteorologists know what will happen tomorrow, the next day, or even a week from today?

As you already know, the atmosphere is a complex system that is constantly in motion. It is not easy to predict the weather! Meteorologists invented most of the basic weather-forecasting tools hundreds of years ago. Today we have many high-tech tools to help us as well. Long-term weather forecasts have become much more accurate than they were in the past.

Weather station

To find out the temperature, humidity, and wind speeds higher in the atmosphere, meteorologists send **weather balloons** into the sky. Just like some birthday balloons, the weather balloon is filled with helium. Helium is a gas that is lighter than air, so it allows the balloon to rise. A weather balloon carries a measuring tool called a **radiosonde.** The radiosonde is able to send data to meteorologists on the ground.

As the balloon goes up, the air pressure around it decreases. The balloon expands and expands. Then, at a certain height, it pops! Bigger balloons can rise higher than smaller ones. Once a weather balloon pops, the radiosonde falls back to Earth with a parachute. Then the device can be picked up and used again.

Weather balloon with a radiosonde

A radar station

There are also many weather **radar** stations around the world. Radar stations send bursts of radio waves into the atmosphere. When the **waves** hit raindrops or snowflakes, the waves **echo** back to the station. Computers process these echoes and create radar maps that help meteorologists understand the size and location of storms. Portable radar devices can be carried by trucks to brewing storms. These devices provide information about storms, including how fast they are moving and in what direction.

Satellites in orbit around the Earth track the size and movement of storms from high above our planet. Cameras in the satellites are constantly sending images back to Earth. Scanning **radiometers** are built into many weather satellites. These instruments can sense the amount of heat given off by the Earth in different places.

The GOES 13 satellite orbiting the Earth

Data from weather stations, radiosondes, and radar can be combined with data from satellites. This huge amount of information gets fed into a giant computer network. The computers process all the data. They compare that day's observations with observations meteorologists have recorded in the past. Using complex mathematical models, they predict the weather from a week to two weeks ahead. Meteorologists access the computer network and look at big global weather patterns. They use the data to make their local forecasts.

Kids playing in the snow

A rainy afternoon may put an end to your plans for a picnic or a ball game. A snowy morning may mean a day off from school. Rainy, windy, and snowy times are part of our everyday weather here on Earth. But sometimes weather takes a dangerous turn! Meteorologists are always on the alert, in case things start to look bad. Stormy weather can destroy trees, cars, and even buildings. It is a sad fact that tornadoes, hurricanes, and other violent storms also kill hundreds of people every year. Meteorologists work hard to warn people when dangerous storms are forming. They help people understand what to do when a storm is approaching so they can stay safe.

With a special radio receiver, you can tune in to the National Weather Service's NOAA Weather Radio for quick access to active weather watches and warnings!

Thunderstorms and Tornadoes

You've probably felt it before—it's a hot summer afternoon, and the air seems very still. A billowy white cloud is growing taller and taller overhead. As it reaches its tallest point, you may see it flatten at the top. Before long, the whole sky grows dark and threatening. Suddenly, you feel a gust of cool wind. You see a flash of **lightning** in the distance. Seconds later, you hear a rumble of **thunder.**

Thornado creates tremendous amounts of noise.

A thundercloud

What's happening? The warm, moist air around you is rising. As the warm air rises, it cools. The water vapor in the air condenses, creating a big, billowy cumulus cloud. If there's enough warm, moist air, it keeps rising and adding to the cloud. The cloud grows bigger and darker. It turns into a threatening cumulonimbus cloud. It may grow so high that it bumps up against the lower level of the stratosphere. This causes the cloud's top to flatten out.

Inside the cloud, water droplets are growing into drops. Soon a few big raindrops fall. The falling rain drags the cooled air down with it.

You feel the cool wind, and before you know it, heavy rain is pouring down. Lightning is flashing and thunder is roaring all around you. You are in a **thunderstorm**!

A stroke of lightning is a giant spark of electricity that forms between two parts of a thundercloud, or between a cloud and the ground. You can think of it like the spark that sometimes zaps you when you shuffle across a rug and then touch a doorknob. The difference is that a doorknob zap is tiny—only about a millimeter long and as thin as a thread. A stroke of lightning, on the other hand, can be up to six miles (ten kilometers) long and more than an inch (three centimeters) thick. One big lightning bolt can have enough **electrical energy** to power a small town for a whole day. Lightning is so hot, it causes the air around it to expand rapidly, or explode. That explosion of air causes the big boom of thunder.

Even though a lightning flash and its thunder boom happen at the same time, you usually see the lightning first and hear the thunder later. That's because light travels faster than sound.

Lightning strikes can be extremely dangerous. If you hear thunder rumbling, go indoors or get inside a car immediately. If you're far away from any cars or buildings, squat as low to the ground as you can. Avoid being the tallest thing in the landscape because that can make you a target for lightning. In an open field, never take shelter under a tree. Trees and other tall objects can act as **lightning rods,** conducting electricity straight from the sky to the ground—where you are!

A Skrill dragon channels lightning down its metallic spine and showers destructive blasts!

In the colder, higher parts of a large thundercloud, ice crystals sometimes form instead of raindrops. If the force of the rising air in the cloud is strong enough, those crystals don't fall right away. As they're tossed around and juggled by the cloud's winds, more and more ice freezes around them. The crystals grow larger and larger until finally they fall— as **hail**! Most hailstones range from pea-sized to golf ball–sized. But much larger hailstones have been recorded.

We sometimes have hailstorms in Berk!

Most thunderstorms don't last much longer than a few hours. But if there's a lot of warm, moist air around, they can grow bigger and last longer. If the upward-moving warm air and downward-moving cool air are creating strong up and down winds, and if there is a strong wind blowing across the upper part of the cloud, the cloud may begin to rotate. When a gigantic thunderstorm begins to rotate, it becomes a **supercell.**

Supercells are very dramatic. They can form anywhere that thunderstorms form. But they are most common in the central United States, where warm, moist air from the Gulf of Mexico meets cooler, dryer air moving down from the north. When meteorologists see a supercell forming, they issue an alert. That's because the world's most destructive tornadoes are born in supercells!

A **tornado** is a narrow, fast-swirling column of wind. Tornado watchers are often the first to spot a small, funnel-shaped cloud forming at the bottom of a supercell. Not all funnel clouds reach the ground, but many do. When they do, the fierce wind pulls in nearby dirt and debris. Trees, cars, houses—any objects in the path of the tornado can get swept up and destroyed.

The wind speed in the most powerful tornadoes can reach over 300 miles per hour (480 kilometers per hour). That's more than four times as fast as a car speeding along an open highway. Most tornadoes have a width between 500 and 2,000 feet (150 and 600 meters). The average tornado is

A tornado forming from a supercell

about as wide as three and a half football fields, placed end zone to end zone. And tornadoes move along the ground at around thirty miles per hour (forty-five kilometers per hour). That's why it's important to stay out of a tornado's path. A tornado moves faster than the fastest human in the world can run!

As soon as meteorologists at the **National Weather Service (NWS)** see that conditions are right for severe thunderstorms, they issue a **tornado watch.** That means the area could soon be having strong winds, lightning, heavy rain, and maybe even hail. These are the conditions in which a tornado could form. Luckily, very few thunderstorms actually spawn tornadoes.

You get a lot of wind power from dragons' wings!

If a funnel cloud forms, a **tornado warning** is issued. Any people in its path are in danger. **Tornado sirens** go off. Radio and television stations broadcast warnings. Everyone in the area is told to take shelter immediately.

The deadliest tornado in U.S. history happened on March 18, 1925. Often called the Tri-State Tornado, it traveled 219 miles (350 kilometers) through Missouri, Illinois, and Indiana. By the time the first main tornado was over, 695 people were dead. Later that day, more tornadoes arrived. They caused even more death and destruction.

Ruins of a Baptist church in Murphysboro, Illinois, destroyed by the Tri-State Tornado

ON JULY 13, 2004, A TORNADO HIT WOODFORD COUNTY, ILLINOIS. It completely destroyed the Parsons Company's manufacturing plant. One hundred forty people were working at the plant that day. All of them survived! The factory's restrooms had been reinforced to act as tornado shelters. Employees had been trained as **storm spotters,** and they had practiced tornado drills twice a year. As soon as one of the storm spotters saw the tornado coming, he warned the others. All the workers got to the shelters in time.

Tornado Safety

When a warning is issued, get to a tornado shelter or storm shelter immediately. If there is no shelter nearby, move to a basement or interior room in a sturdy building. Stay away from doors and windows. Use a mattress or thick blankets to protect yourself from falling debris. Check out the website below to learn more about tornado and thunderstorm safety!

http://www.nws.noaa.gov/os/severeweather/

Today, meteorologists have better tornado detection tools and more effective warning systems than they had in the past. Many more **tornado shelters** have been built in areas likely to have tornadoes. Schoolchildren in these areas have **tornado drills,** much like the fire drills all schools have. Knowing what to do in an emergency helps save lives!

Everyone in Berk works together!

Hurricanes and Blizzards

Before satellites and radar were invented, it was almost impossible for people to be sure when a violent storm was on its way. In 1900, Galveston was one of the biggest cities in Texas. During the first week of September that year, the people of Galveston were enjoying nice, sunny weather. Families were swimming in the warm ocean water at the city's beach.

Then, on September 7, meteorologists in Galveston noticed the ocean waves were much larger than usual. Big clouds were moving in fast. The meteorologists recognized these danger signs and hung red-and-black hurricane-warning flags. A storm was approaching!

The next morning, many people checked the skies. It was cloudy and spritzy and the tide was unusually high, but they were used to such weather in Galveston.

Hurricane-warning flags

They decided the weather didn't look that bad and went back to the beach. Meteorologists had become quite worried at this point, of course. That afternoon, a violent wind began to slam the coast. It shattered windows and ripped the roofs off houses. Heavy rain blew sideways in the wind. A wide, high dome of

Raincutter dragons would like hurricanes because they forage in the rain!

ocean water called a **storm surge** swept through the town. Whole city blocks were washed away. By the time the storm passed, over 8,000 people had lost their lives. It was the deadliest hurricane in U.S. history.

Hurricanes are huge, rotating storms. They form over warm ocean water—a great source of the warm, moist air hurricanes need to fuel them! A hurricane's winds spiral in toward its center. The wind speeds can reach anywhere from 74 to over 155 miles per hour (119 to over 250 kilometers per hour). At the center of every hurricane is a calm area of low pressure, known as the **eye.** Most hurricanes are between 60 and 930 miles (100 and 1,500 kilometers) wide. These are the most destructive storms on the planet!

HURRICANE SANDY pounded the United States' East Coast in 2012. It was 945 miles (1,520 kilometers) wide. That's almost the whole distance from Massachusetts to Georgia! Sandy was one of the widest hurricanes ever measured.

HURRICANE KATRINA

In August 2005, Hurricane Katrina became the deadliest storm in recent U.S. history. The high winds alone destroyed thousands of houses and other buildings along the Gulf Coast. But that was not the worst problem. The hurricane caused a storm surge twenty-three feet (seven meters) high! The surge broke through flood walls designed to keep the city of New Orleans, Louisiana, from flooding. Not long after the hurricane had passed over, most of New Orleans was underwater. Early hurricane warnings helped hundreds of thousands of people **evacuate** before the storm hit. Even so, more than 1,800 people lost their lives.

Most of the hurricanes that hit the East Coast and Gulf Coast of the United States take place in the summer or early fall. They form north of the equator, over the Atlantic Ocean. As summer heat grows, vast amounts of warm, moist air begin to rise. This causes groups of severe thunderstorms to form. The Earth's rotation creates the Coriolis force, which can set these storms swirling.

If the swirling winds reach thirty-nine miles per hour (sixty-three kilometers per hour), a severe thunderstorm becomes something more serious. It becomes a **tropical storm.** Meteorologists give the storm a name. They watch it closely on radar and satellite images. If the winds reach seventy-four miles per hour (119 kilometers per hour), the tropical storm is categorized as a hurricane.

- Scientists call a hurricane a tropical cyclone. It's called "tropical" because it forms in the tropics—areas just north or south of the equator. **"Cyclone"** comes from the Greek word **kyklon,** meaning "whirling."
- "Hurricane" comes from the name of the ancient Mayan storm god, Huracan.
- In the northwestern Pacific, tropical cyclones are called typhoons.
- In the southwestern Pacific and the Indian Ocean, these storms are called cyclones.

HURRICANE SAFETY

Check out the National Weather Service website below to learn more about hurricane safety!
nws.noaa.gov/om/hurricane

Meteorologists use every tool they have to figure out which path a hurricane is likely to take. Will it hit the coast? Or will it veer off and miss the coast entirely? The path of a hurricane is difficult to predict, but satellite and radar images and advanced computer models make meteorologists' predictions much better than they were in the time of the Galveston hurricane.

If it looks like hurricane conditions may hit an area, the National Weather Service issues a **hurricane watch.** If a hurricane is expected, a **hurricane warning** is issued thirty-six hours before landfall. This allows people enough time to secure their homes and safely leave the area.

Did you know many of Berk's dragons are named after weather?

Air Force hurricane-hunting aircraft

The Hurricane Hunters are brave U.S. Air Force scientists. They fly directly into hurricanes to collect weather data. Check out the following website to learn more about the Hurricane Hunters!
hurricanehunters.com

Trains stuck outside New York City's Grand Central Terminal during the Great Blizzard of 1888

Swirling storms that begin in cooler areas, away from the tropics, are mid-latitude cyclones. In cold weather, these cyclones can become **blizzards.** Blizzards are winter storms with huge amounts of blowing snow and high winds of at least thirty-five miles per hour (fifty-six kilometers per hour).

In the United States, along the north Atlantic coast, one of the most feared winter storms is the **nor'easter.** A nor'easter is a big storm that blows along this coast, with swirling winds from the northeast. The Great Blizzard of 1888 was a nor'easter that dumped nearly sixty inches (1.5 meters) of snow on parts of New York, New Jersey, Connecticut, Massachusetts, and Rhode Island. In

New York City, fierce winds blew the fallen snow into drifts that were high enough to cover second-story windows. Some people froze to death in the streets. Outside the city, many houses were completely buried in snowdrifts. Winds reached eighty miles per hour (129 kilometers per hour). Telegraph wires blew down, trains could not move, and people were stuck in their homes for many days.

In the Great Blizzard of 1993, a combination of freezing temperatures, high winds, and blowing snow fell across a huge area—starting from the southeastern United States all the way north into eastern Canada. Storm surges flooded hundreds of communities on the Gulf Coast. More than ten million households lost electricity. Roads and airports were closed. Many people called it the storm of the century.

Berk is always stormy and cold!

With the help of our modern, high-tech tools and lots of experience, the National Weather Service (NWS) was able to issue blizzard warnings two days before the storm arrived. This allowed people time to stock up on emergency supplies before the storm hit. The Blizzard of 1993 is a great example of how far we've come in preparing to keep ourselves and others safe from natural disasters.

When winter winds blow, it's best to stay home! Always pay attention to severe storm watches and warnings. Plan ahead, and stay safe!

WINTER STORM SAFETY

Check out the website below to learn more about winter storm safety!
nws.noaa.gov/om/winter/before.shtml

Man the fort, Hiccup!

Floods and Droughts

People need rain. It makes our crops grow, and it provides water for our farm animals. It fills our wells and reservoirs so we all have fresh water to drink. After many days of heat and sunshine, the patter of rain on a rooftop is a welcome sound. But sometimes rain can become dangerous.

The winter of 2007–2008 was very snowy across most of the midwestern United States. When spring came, the snow melted, causing the ground to become wet and mushy. People in Iowa, Wisconsin, Indiana, and Illinois worried that the usual spring rains would make the ground even wetter. But things were about to get much wetter than they ever expected. Spring came, and it rained and rained. By the end of May, lawns looked like swamps. Basements had become wet and clammy. Everywhere, streams and rivers were flowing high and fast. People felt as if the rain would never stop!

June arrived, and the rain continued. In Martinsville, Indiana, meteorologists measured over 20 inches (about 510 millimeters) of rain during that month alone. That was twice as much rain as anyone had ever seen there in a single month.

The National Guard responding to the flood in Martinsville, Indiana

Water flooded over millions of acres of farmland. Crops were ruined. In many towns near the rivers, people had to leave their homes. In Cedar Rapids, Iowa, more than four hundred city blocks were underwater. Gradually the rains slowed down. But it was many weeks before things were back to normal.

Floods like the Midwestern Flood of 2008 are part of the natural way rivers and streams behave. Whenever there is a lot of precipitation over an area for a long time, rivers and streams rise. When the amount of water grows too great, it will spill over onto the land. During flood times, anyone who lives close to a river or stream can be in danger. Engineers build dams across rivers and streams to hold water back. They build **levees** along the banks of rivers to keep floodwater in the rivers and away from towns.

DID YOU KNOW?

- Just six inches (fifteen centimeters) of fast-moving water can knock a person down!
- Most cars and trucks can be swept away in only two feet (0.6 meters) of rushing water!

Washed-out roads during 2013 Colorado floods

Some of the scariest floods are **flash floods**. These fast-moving floods happen in mountainous or hilly areas. Over a very short time—usually a few hours—a huge amount of rain falls. Water flows down a mountain's sides and turns into a roaring wall of water. Flash floods cover a relatively small area—tearing down buildings, uprooting trees, and washing away roads and bridges. While large-area floods can last for weeks, flash floods happen quickly. Water levels often return to normal within a few hours, revealing the terrible destruction left behind.

What's the opposite of too much rain? No rain at all! A **drought** is a stretch of weather that is so dry, it hurts crops and leaves people without enough water for everyday use.

In California's Central Valley, winter is the rainy season. The winter of 2011–2012 was very dry. The next winter was dry, and the winter after that, too. The winter of 2014–2015 was one of the driest in that area since people began keeping records in 1849.

The rolling hills of California's Central Valley in dry weather

Most of California's fruits and vegetables are grown in the Central Valley. During the dry months of summer, farmers depend on lakes and reservoirs to help water their crops. Normally, those bodies of water get refilled every winter by rainfall. But after four dry winters, they became dangerously low. California was in an extreme drought! When any area is suffering from a drought, people are asked to cut back on their water use. This is called **water restrictions** and allows for only important uses of water, like drinking and bathing.

We have no problem NOT bathing!

People aren't allowed to water their lawns or wash their cars. But much worse than that—the soil dries out and crops die. Farm animals have to be sent to other areas where there is enough water.

THE DUST BOWL

In the late 1800s and early 1900s, many families settled in the area of the central United States called the Great Plains. These people plowed the land and planted crops such as wheat, corn, and cotton. During the 1930s, much less rain fell on the Great Plains than usual, causing a terrible drought. The drought hit parts of Oklahoma, Texas, Kansas, Colorado, and New Mexico the hardest.

As a result, crops withered and died. Large areas of land lay bare and brown. When the wind blew, it picked up tons of loose, dry soil. Dark, billowing clouds of dirt and dust filled the air. The dust got into people's eyes, noses, and mouths, making it hard to see and breathe. No one was safe from these dust storms. Millions of people had no choice but to pack up their things and leave their homes. Thousands went hungry and homeless.

People called the dust storms black blizzards. The area was nicknamed the Dust Bowl. Later, that became the name of this tragic event.

Years later, many farmers moved back to the area. They learned to farm in ways that preserved the soil and kept it from blowing away. They planned ahead for future droughts.

When a drought goes on for a long time, even deep underground wells begin to dry up. People then face serious water shortages. Sometimes they have to leave their homes and find new places to live!

Southern California wildfires

When an area is in a drought, trees, bushes, and grasses dry out. A bolt of lightning can cause them to catch fire. Sometimes people are careless with campfires or while burning trash. Fire can spread quickly to dried-out plants. **Wildfires** are large areas of fast-spreading, uncontrolled fire.

DROUGHT AND WILDFIRE SAFETY

Check out the National Weather Service websites below to learn more about drought and wildfire safety!
nws.noaa.gov/om/drought • nws.noaa.gov/om/fire/index.shtml

They often occur in forests and grasslands. But when they happen near homes and businesses, they can be extremely dangerous.

Between 1995 and 2009, wide areas of Australia experienced their worst drought ever recorded. During that time, wild, uncontrolled fires in the bush and forests, called **bushfires,** raged across much of the landscape.

WEATHER VS. CLIMATE: WHAT'S THE DIFFERENCE?

An area's **weather** changes from day to day and from season to season. An area's **climate** is its average weather over a long period of time.

All of us live on planet Earth, in an ever-moving ocean of air. Our weather is always changing. Weather emergencies like the Dust Bowl and Hurricane Katrina become part of our history. Families pass down their own storm stories to their children and grandchildren. Meteorologists gather and record as much information as possible. Understanding the storms of the past can help us figure out what to do in the future, whenever a storm is approaching!

It's important to learn about weather because it affects our everyday lives—even if it's just a matter of knowing to bring sunscreen or an umbrella with us when we step out of the house. But it's also good to know what kind of extreme weather you may occasionally expect in your part of the country, and what to do in the event that weather turns dangerous. Being aware and prepared is just smart! But don't worry too much, because there are always people and systems in place to help keep you safe.

Now we know all about weather. On to the next adventure!